Singing at the Center

Terre Ouwehand

Old Hand Press
Santa Barbara, California

Art by Pamela Zwehl-Burke

Cover Image: Petroglyph I, 6"x8" watercolor, 2010

Interior Images: Singing, 6"x6" charcoal, 2005 (bowl); Holding, 6"x6" graphite, 2009 (frog);
Hole in the Heart III, p. 2, 3"x3" intaglio, 1994 (empty nest); Hole in the Heart III, p. 1, 3"x3" intaglio, 1994 (bird in nest);
Petroglyph II, 6"x8" watercolor, 2010;
Steady, 5"x7" powered graphite, 2004 (candle);
Bud-Bloom-Burst, p. 4, 6"x6" intaglio, 2003 (closed rose); Bud-Bloom-Burst, p. 7, 6"x6" intaglio, 2003 (open rose);
Holding (Shells), 6"x6", charcoal, 2004 (cupped hands);
Petroglyph III, 6"x8" watercolor, 2010

Cover design by Tom Buhl

Fonts: Verdana, Lucida

Library of Congress Control Number 2010910948

ISBN 978-0-9828910-0-1

To

lb

Contents

Trees

Trees
are God's particular sign posts:
They are always pointing in the right direction.

No matter how many
bends, or twists, or turns
a tree must make, it grows always
toward the light.

If you seek gainful employment—
If you desire a purpose in life—
Be a tree.

GNOSIS

Spirit nudges,
silent, blind
subterranean wonder ...

Source shifts,
restless dreamer,
dark, inscrutable mind ...

Sophia rises,
inaudible song
vibrating deep and low,
slow ascent— years, centuries ...

Words pulled up
from primordial silt
crawl up the back of my tongue,
haul themselves forward, immense,

swollen with forbidden wisdom
and abandoned love.

They teach me their forgotten sounds.
They will work me like a tuning fork
to raise the rest from sleep.

Desert Pentecost

Runic stones, sacred clay
lie in the light of this immense
and silent furnace—straw,
sage, dry white air—
Come! Indwell this primal house,
oh, Holy Breath and Fire!

Teach lizard tongue to speak,
cactus mouths gape and shape the word—
lost language of the earth—

Shout enigmatic wonders!
Women and men in cities
are gods for a day
conversant on uncommon ground.

But here is revelation:
writ in star point
on a milky blaze of heaven.

Come then.
Sound this body
with sound unheard,
blast, sweep, lick this flesh house!
Make it howl and sing—
with holy breath and fire.

Covenant

Come
into the desert
and build yourself
a temple—

pound air and light
with clay of your body,
and build—
                    see it rise
hour to hour, brick upon straw,
use blood to glaze the walls
palming the paste in smooth, eternal
                    circles, circles ...

          preserve
          a center
          point:
          where
          the small
          white

blaze
of my eye
burns—
go
into it
often,
touch your tongue
into the flame!
ring your heart
against the altar!
and listen—

Build yourself, a temple—
a tabernacle of silk
and cedar—   thought
to thought, day into day,
translucent, permeable
that I may pass in
and out, in and out—

And I will be your God.

Vital Signs

Earth talks to me:

It throws down twigs in alphabet—

arranges stones, leaves, seaweed

in calligraphic intimations—

whole novels lie underfoot,

treatises, poems!

Wind instructs: Be quiet ...

the air is full of dog-whistles—

I must change my life.

On the Road:
from Joachim's journal

I

The road is dry,
the silence wide,
you are the rose in my heart,
the song in my center.

II

For you I watched.
I waited. I walked. My soul
grew wide, my spirit long.

III

I prepared you a table,
and feasted in my heart.
I made you a bed,
and rested in my soul.
The stars watched,
and you knew.

You were welcomed,
and I was thanked.
You prayed for me,
and at great distance
we both smiled,
we both slept.

IV

Sandals kiss earth, I
inspect the falling sky for signs
of Love's return.

V

Your eyes are the stars
before me, your voice a bell
that beckons me home.

VI

Blue divinity, azure robe
ribboning the world, a
Lover's gift.

Requiem
for Creatures Smaller
than a Cow

Of all the creatures God made before He—
or She—made the cow, the dog and the cat
were especially meant as friends
for humankind. They share our houses,
our beds, our garages, our favorite chairs—
their lairs, and hairs, are everywhere!
More comfort than our children, more
affectionate, and loyal, than our spouses,
they're really the center of our houses
and our lives.
We're just not allowed to admit it.
They'd commit us in an instant, and yet
it is the truth.

We have with them the deepest intimacy,
without recriminations or outrageous
expectations, just acceptance for exactly
who we are.

What relief.

So, in memoriam... dear Pookie, Simon,
Henry Bad-Cat, Snowball, Isadora, Max,
Kate, Neiko, Bogie, Mel, Mo, Bunce, Chester,
Spike, Maggie, Pumpkin, Nisha, Merlin...
and Cleo...
May you rest in peace
in the backyards of our lives.

An Admirable Companion

Cleo was a cat.
A special cat, to be sure.
An admirable companion.
We were together 18 years—
that's a third of my life.

Cleo was distinctive:
She had "piano" toes
She *really* looked at you
She liked to be in the center
She assumed house guests came to see her
She talked—a lot
She had an unusual meow
She sat on laps
She loved being petted.

Cleo was a good cat.
Yes, we had our disputes.
Since I paid the bills I imagined
being in charge. Often I was.

We lived in 3 houses:
We moved from El Capitan (where
she was born) to Carpinteria.
I taught Study Abroad in
Cambridge, England 3 times (they
were semester length: 3 months).
Cleo lived with others, in *her* condo.
She was always glad to see me when
I came home—I can see her trotting down
the stairs, meowing, "Yea! You're home!"

Cleo carried all my projections,
without even knowing it; they had
no weight for her. I take them back,
hoist them onto my shoulders, and feel
no weight. No weight. I smile.

Cleo is with me.
That's us up the road.

Cleo was a cat.
A very special cat.
An admirable companion.

A riff on euphemism
Or
What if Andy Rooney
came to Pamela's show?

"Bit the dust".
What's that taste like?
Are you supposed to swallow?
Will it stick in your teeth?

"Bought the farm".
Was there an open house?
Could you view it online?
Do you pay points?
Can you even get a loan for such a purchase?

"Croak".
Must you squat near a pond?

I think eating flies & bugs
would make *me* croak.

"Passed away".
Is that like passing the butter?
Or passing the wine?
Or passing gas?
Maybe it's like passing your exit
while daydreaming at the wheel.

"Kicked the bucket".
Are there tryouts for this, and
practice after school?
Do they use goal posts?
Do you get a running start?
Or do you have to do it in place?
Is there ever anything *in* the bucket?
Do you get to wear cleats?

"Still Life".
Is it *still* life?
Or is it stopped life?
Or left-over life?
Should you store it in Tupperware
between paintings?

"Breathed his last".
Is that inhaling on the last cigarette
the condemned are offered
in old movies?
Or is that just the last cigarette?
The last mile?
The last supper.
Last farewell.
Last hoorah.
The last word.

[Untitled]

Violet air with black hills,
Light comes, goes, comes ...
We are grass.
Spend your life.

Good Friday, 2006

We waited in the morning sun
trying not to think how the
heat rising in our skins
was slowly boiling his brain,
how his blood was draining from
his torso down into his thighs and
clogging his knee joints.
We tried not to see the small movements
he made attempting to adjust his body
against the pain.

We tried not to look at his mother,
no one spoke,
she never raised her eyes to him.

At midday our own brains felt boiled.
Our mouths tasted dust.
We hoped he was dead.

A cloud drifted in from the desert,

poised for a while overhead. We
prayed for some rain—just
a little, please, God, just a little—and
felt our muscles unclench in a cooling
shadow, but it began to shred and
moved off in clumps.

Someone came up behind us,
whispered to John that Joseph had
begged for his body
and they'd be here before sunset
to take him down
as long as he was dead.

He was dead, all right. We hadn't
seen him even flinch in hours.
He'd had a good physique but
aside from the traveling we hadn't done
regular work for a couple years.
It's just as well he wasn't any stronger.

Someone began to cry and tried hard

to hide it. I ground my teeth, bit
my lip, something to focus, distract.

Others were coming up the hill—I
could hear several pairs of feet walking
steadily over the rocky ground—
perhaps it is Joseph and the soldiers, we
thought, finally meeting each other's eyes.

Then we heard her—weeping, quietly,
into her hijab—weeping in muffled,
ragged breaths.
Our hearts cracked fully,
and we slowly stepped
through the opening.

Good Friday, 2010

And he said: Yes, I am the son of God
and so are you
and you and you and you and
you … pointing at each of us.
Everyone is the son or daughter of God.
Everyone
is the child of God.
I came forth to make this clear
but Christianity has made me the ONLY son
of God—THE son of God—of the same
substance with the Father.
He shrugged his shoulders and sighed and
added: We all came from God's substance.

And I said: I am the blue-robed figure!
He focused on me, our eyes lighted, he
gave a little nod. And he smiled.

Good Friday, 2000

You spared me the worst of it.
Set me and sent me off to make the next
arrangements—even though you knew
there would be none,
none beyond this last stay
in Jerusalem.

By the time I got back
it was all done, all over:
I heard the stories, saw
the places where blood had dropped.
Then I walked out over the far road that
leads to the killing hill—
fresh sacrifices hang there now.

You *let* them take you,
and my sorrow is all for myself.
How will I complete this teaching?
How will I accomplish this thing
without you: my door, my heart,

my friend, my lord ...?

I touched you, Joachim,
touch others.
That is how you complete
the teaching.
Spend your life
that you shall not lose it.
It is easy to love when
the Beloved is beside you.
The trial is
to love when he is gone.
Thoroughly, utterly gone.

And this is how you must learn
to love God. Manifest being is
sheathed, and your desire is
foiled; as if wearing heavy gloves
you tried to touch the skin of
your Beloved—
your fingertips remember, dimly,
so vaguely the memory feels
imagined, invented, the subtle
chimera of longing only ...

I tell you the way is to foster,
nurse that ephemeral intimation.
Make it a song, so indistinct
it is impossible to recall
completely,
full of spaces, murmurs,
yet be determined to one day
sing!
          Listen—
listen in the silence and the din,
for another note, a syllable ...

This is how you finish
the teaching
we began so long ago.

To Calvary, Good Friday, 1995

Who are you?
That drags me from my bed
at 4 a.m., pushes me
up a hill—steep but hardly
Golgatha—a quite safe, even
desirable neighborhood, in
the moonlit pre-dawn
of dogs and other urban creatures;
easy in sturdy shoes and
woolen warmed against a
cool spring breeze,
carrying a couple of sticks
and a flashlight ...
sleepy, reluctant muscles,
but, really, not much the less
for wear—

Who am I?
To mask the pilgrim,
dissemble the Cyrene, or
Veronica, or young John—

What can I know?
When sleep and breakfast are all
I sacrifice—
What can I know
about flesh receiving nails?
(What can I possibly know?)

My soul lies in shallow snow,
burned once by your sudden kiss
ashes breathe.

Good Friday, 2009

I would like to do something,
deny myself something,
make things harder,
but I am thinking (this year) about
the Good ...
What? Why?

Perhaps he went joyfully,
certainly he seems to have gone willingly.
It is a hard door to open—painful—
though one may have friends near, supportive,
empathetic, it's not their experience—
that door must be opened alone,
and walked through alone—that part is
hard—going to an unknown place,
choosing to open an unknown door and
walking through an unknown doorway—
no one can know until it happens to them—
and it will happen to us all—we will all die—
we all have to do this. Emergence

is often experienced as emergency.
How will I experience it?

I feel some tears well up: perhaps that gives me a clue as to why I always cry when I think of Jesus' Crucifixion ... maybe I am crying for myself, the little me who was crucified—it was unbelievably painful—I felt alone—the people closest to me, my mother and my father, were the reason I was being crucified!

All was split (like the temple curtain).
All was dreadfully coming apart
(like the earthquake).
And all the buried bodies were coming forth
from their graves.

My mother and father were so in their own pain
they could not see how enormous was mine.
So big I could not carry it (the Cyrene).
I was too small. I was too small.
So Jesus carried me.

And I died in his arms.

"It is finished," he said.

II

I was resurrected.
It was a hard door to open.
It took years.

I think I feel—joy—
which I did not believe I would ever feel.
Joy.
I can better understand the apostles'
enthusiasm: they were joyful.

This has been a long journey.
Images and metaphors were (and are)
the preparation for going through a door.
A doorway that must be walked through
alone.
I do feel different:
lighter, more porous.
Jesus is laughing,
again.

Creation IV

Fire and vapor
churning,
mixing,
cooling,
pooling …
methane mud,
microbial mouths
sucking,
sleeping—

Vibration
tickling the silt,
God's footfall—
wind in the garden,
breath in the leaves—
steaming,
settling,
greening
awake …

And the generations
of Earth were these:
Cyanophyte begat Protozoa
who begat Anemone who begat
Limpet, Whelk and Trilobite
who begat Lacewing Fly
and Pink Flower Mantis
who begat Sea Squirt who
begat Coelacanth who begat
Iguana and Sidewinder
who begat Egret and Eagle
who begat Platypus who begat
Shrew and Sloth who begat
Dolphin, Buffalo, Impala and Bear,
Lemur, Loris and Macaque ...

Love
thrusting into clay
rising
dreaming
aware
and a wonder!

Even if he were not

Even if he were not
divine—(in the technical sense—
not supernatural)—he was
the highest we can go,
and he raised the clay in us
up toward something finer,
breathed his spirit into us,
and we felt whole
and real.
That is miracle enough.

He embodied for a moment
our dream of God: the cosmos
come into our tents and seated at our tables—
to show us a face, to care, to touch,
to disclose the immaculate latency of creation.

For these alone
he is worthy of our thanks and praise.

Madonna

Out of the womb of Midnight Ether:

Art

        And asteroid –

Beauty

                And bone –

                        Compassion

And chromium –

                Desire

                        And DNA –

Elegance

                And elephant –

                        Fertility

And fire –

                Geometry

And giraffe –

                        Heaven

And hyacinth –

                Identity –

                        And ice –

Justice

                And juniper –

Kinship

And kidney –

Logos

And lily –

Memory

And magnet –

Necessity

And neuron –

Offering

And orbit –

Perception

And pear –

Quantum

And quasar –

Reverence

And radium –

Syllogism

And seagull –

Truth

And twilight –

Union

And umber –

Vigilance

And velvet worm –

Warmth

And wave –

Yearning

And yeast –

Zero

And zygote –

And God saw
all that She had made,
and loved it.
And therefore
set it free.

Trafficking in God

–Monastery of the Redwoods, Whitethorn

Go to the woods and knock.
Stand at the gate of the sky and call.
Shout till you are heard!
It will open.
The world is smudged with divine fingerprints.
Every Thing is a sign-post, a signal. This way—
Slow— Construction Zone Ahead— Yield—
Enter—
The Redwoods are a cathedral:
Elegant giants compel your eyes upward,
columns sway like bodies dreaming,
high leaves fracture the light, multi-
formed, multi-planed, sparkling transoms,
the filigree of ferns, and the silent-soled
attendance of delicate wing and subtle claw.
My heart kneels, my body prays.
Earth is a temple.
We serve every day.

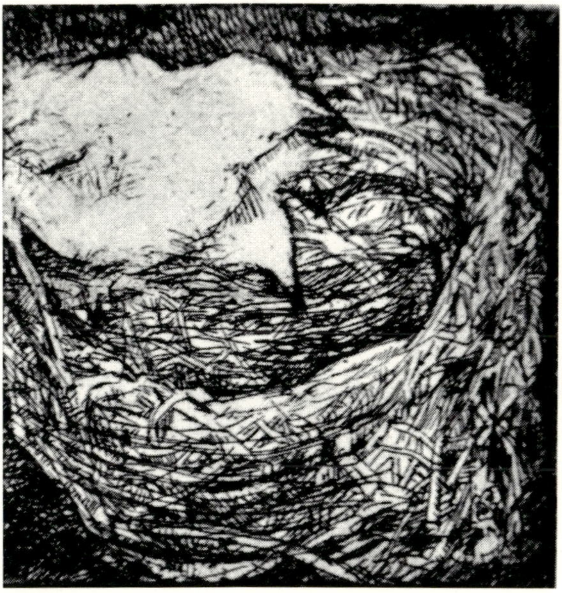

From

The Divorce Museum,

a Child's Perspective

a poem cycle

PROLOGUE

Over 51% of marriages in the United States
fail.
Now if 51% of, say, Wendy's hamburgers or
Ford trucks failed—if they made you sick or
ran you off the road more than half the time—
you can be sure
the appropriate state or federal agency would
shut them down, put them out of business!
But I guess with marriage the government,
at any level, figures, well, they're only hurting
themselves.

Ah.
If it were only so.

I remember the day that I was driving with
my brother down to Key West,
and he said to me,
"Our childhood was not actually so great,
was it?"
The skies parted!

Heroic film music rose around me!
Yes! Yes, I shouted inside my head
(above the musical score)
someone else is saying that!

It had been hard for so many years—
we were not kids on this little jaunt down
the Keys, but adults in our late 30s and early
40s. No one believed that any real harm
had been sustained.
It had been hard to be the only one willing
to admit (not verbally, mind you, but by the
act of going into therapy) that I was
not actually so great ...

Now I had someone (or at least the prospect
of someone—we'd have to see how far this
revelation would go) to help carry it, this
massive thing that did not exist.

And I thought, someday maybe I could even
show him a very secret room that has
attached itself to every house
I've lived in,
with its trap door under every relationship,
where a drama not my own is played out
and yet
is absolutely mine ...

Someday I will take him through my
Divorce Museum,
where I have hung the pictures I have made
of the moments
when we were small
and living in a life that was not our life
and would always be absolutely ours.

The House on Richardson Road

I swung into the house
careening on the gust of a summer
back porch door slam—
I was six.
The kitchen was quiet and dim.
The warm still air outside
clanked periodically
with the mechanical sounds my father
emitted from beneath his tan and white Chevy.

From the hall I could see my mother passing
inside her bedroom doorway, back
and forth, from the bureau to the bed.
There's nothing the matter with dreams,
she would say.
Except that they take you away
from the people you love.
She was already gone.

I watched, undisclosed
in the summer shadows, listening
to his mechanic's tapping and
clanging forge their final impasse.

Some years later she returned.
But I never saw again the woman who stood
folding tears into a suitcase.

Untitled, Wire and Marble

How can you let us go?

He sat awkwardly between us
on the big couch in Grandma's
living room, repeating
what we'd already heard long-distance:
We were going to live with Mom again,
in Los Angeles, with a new dad.

We don't need a new dad.
We need you.

We didn't fidget. We sat
heavy and stiff, like bookends
propping him up.
We couldn't believe
he was giving in, giving
up, giving us away—
to some guy we'd never met.
Why didn't he fight for us?
Why didn't he love us?

I'll always be your dad, he said.
I'll always love you.

We stood at the screen door,
stolid, watched him stride down the porch,
descend the steps, cross the sidewalk
and climb into his new jeep.
He started the motor,
then looked at us—
and just kept looking, his hand still
resting on the ignition.
Then he drove out of our lives.

We didn't cry.
We were turned to stone.

Reunion: We are 4 and 8

The bluntness of our need
makes her recede from us
as if giving in to its tide
would be sure drowning.

We, on the other hand, are so full
of holes by now we float!
like whiffle-balls
you can throw all day to the waves
and they keep bobbing and rolling back,
and by their persistent presence
ask to be picked up, carried, played with ...

Her absence—now 3 years,
and we are only 4 and 8—is such
lead inside her that she stands at the waterline
where our lives have been rejoined, and
buried instinct warns her she would
not survive the depths of our desire.

Zombie Nights

The Body Snatchers returned us
to the point of our abduction
(when she went away, she made our
dad go somewhere else; *everyone*
disappeared)

but we were only three now
and relocated across the country
and we were supposed to believe
that everything was just as it was.

Our Single Mother Unit
worked hard
to have her glamorous career (in
transportation) and her Child Units at
the same time. We lived in an apartment
(overlooking a freeway). She
programmed us to be helpful, to be
good. We performed adequately.

We forgot about the pods
moldering in the car port storage bin.

We grew new flesh
and pressed it against each other.
And believed this love was the real thing.
The zomboids inside us liquified,
emulsified till we believed we were
actually
who we had been.

We blended in, we passed
so well that even we did not
remember that this was not
our true home.

Loser

I am a loser.
Not in the colloquial sense,
for actually I look like a *haver*—
  I have a nice job, house, friends—
No,
I have a pattern of losing more
serious, esoteric things:

I keep losing my parents.
It's not that I misplace them,
it's not I who am careless,
they disappear of their own accord.
The first time was when I was 6
and they dissolved right in front of me
into an oblivion they called Divorce;
  they phoned in periodically—
with them they must have taken
my "trust fund", which I now believe
contained essential instructions
on how to be content, cultivate

joy, celebrate, love ... I can't seem
to hold onto these very long either.

After some years one of them showed up again!
like a silver dollar wedged beneath the agitator
of an old washing machine, an unexpected and
nostalgic prize; the other though was like
the proverbial sock—subsequent launderings
never returned it, yet we kept the mate for
years just in case ...

Decades later
when I was old enough to say I minded
they lost themselves again—
to be precise, of course, they were not
the *exact* individuals but a permutation
via remarriage—

This time they took with them
the help I needed to be an adult,
from mating to mortgages they nicked
the manuals and I was left again to
figure things out on my own ...

I lose lovers like sunglasses
and the aptitude for home-repair sticks
with me about as long as a mental grocery list.

I keep losing my will to live—
that sounds so dramatic, I know,
but what I mean is that my will to
   achieve, aspire, connect, create, do
                    is
feeble, inconsistent, unreliable;
again, it's not that I'm heedless,
in fact, I'm quite attentive, I
just don't know where it goes ...
   I imagine it oxidizing, rusting
somewhere on the patio ...
evaporating, floating away on the slightest
breeze, or melting into redwood floor boards
or cement, inextricable, irretrievable ...

Limping Toward Bethlehem

I've heard that there are wonders
which break, with some awkwardly
envisioned regularity, into this world.

I even used to trade in such
signs and wonders, making expressions
those visionaries eagerly employed
as confirmations, or at least advertisements.

But one day I woke on a battlefield
diorama—for the betrayal of intimacy
is annihilation, and the denial of innocence
is desecration—and I
believed it was the whole world. And
it was penetratingly clear that no such
wonders could ever have broken into
this, and any visionary I had ever entertained
was a charlatan
or delusional, and I was a fool.

I wrapped myself in my despair
and gave myself to the jaws of darkness.

Years passed.
I lived like a submarine.

Then something else happened.
I'm told that I was found in a
field hospital somewhere on the murky
boundaries of the gray, skull-green
horizon of my old diorama.

Putting on fresh clothes is like
suddenly remembering that I was born.
The lightly starched cloth keeps me upright
and I try to walk. I try to see
to the end of the hallway
and wonder if I will be in a nursing
home for the rest of what I think is
my life.

In this winter season
I limp toward Bethlehem
expecting nothing
but clean straw to lie down in,
and the strange assurance of
creatures who do not
contemplate their lives,
who do not know death until it comes.

WINTER SOLSTICE

There is a place in the soul
Where the longest night of the year
Finds familiar lodging, a place
Of deep and winter and an odd
Kind of darkness turns the landscape
A dense, absorbing blue:
Movement is silent as a photograph,
Air is thin as thought ...

A chord of memory buried in the spine
Wonders, Will we last till daylight?
The horns and claws of a human life
Prowling at the entrances to consciousness—

There is nothing to do
But sit, looking for your own
Hand in front of your face
Through the thick black dark
In the cave of the heart where
The Self sleeps, dreamless and still.

The Very Tidy House

Part I

There's a dead body
on the floor of our living room.
It's been there, oh, 40 odd years.
It's me, at about age 7.
It lies there, dead center, and everyone
steps over and around it as if it were
not even a wrinkle in the carpet;
yet I am sure, dead confident in fact, that
one day they will notice
and I will get my life back—
they *will* rescue me—it's only
a matter of time, and though I am
not patient, I am faithful.

My little brother has rolled under a hassock;
it's far less clear that he is dead
(he was so young when it all happened)
they may think he is napping, but I
am clearly, unavoidably deceased.

Part II

Yesterday I got up—threw in the towel—
they have not noticed this either.
Everything is tidy, no need to straighten
the carpet: there is no lump, no wrinkle,
never was.

I am incredibly annoyed that such a masterful act
of performance art has gone unappreciated.
Think of the other work I might have produced!

The Lost God

When I was 7, I exiled God
from the bombed-out ruins of my
annihilated universe.

I lay awake night after night in the upstairs
front bedroom after my grandmother's
house had fallen asleep,
muffled into blankets and pillow and the remains
of my still-loyal tribe of stuffed animals,
        I cried,
I pleaded with Him to bring my mother home
and to return my dad to the man I'd
always known.
She was *so* far away.
        I prayed:
        Keep her safe.
        Bring her home.

I guess he did the first.

Years later when she did come back for us
I no longer ascribed the event to
any act of intervention.
He no longer existed.

In my 20s, I used the word "God"
like a cockshuttle, whacked it over
intellectual nets in academic competitions—
synonymed it with "Crutch", spurned those
who substituted it for the Good Parent they
didn't have.

I was tempted, sure,
but not deceived.

When I was 30-something, I lost the only
creature I'd learned to love openly, and
I believed the pain would kill me.
        I cried
in the arms of a more or less still-loyal lover,
and feared death so fully I could not live
in my skin.

I spent years descending the stairs
from that old front bedroom, long, dark
passages—carrying my life in laundry bags
destined for the basement where Grandma
still worked over her washer and ringer
and drying lines.
Long, dark passages.
Every time I thought there could be no further
down, more stairs appeared.
There was even a place below the cellar, below
the cement foundation—I swam among graves
so subterranean they were not in any archive.

God, or someone-something like Him, made
occasional, dramatic cameo appearances in this
my psychic morass: my suspicious, vigilant ego
explained them away to my reductive satisfaction
as it caulked the seams along which entry may
have been gained.

And now, so many years and psychic miles
beyond, and 50 just a few blocks and a corner
or two ahead, I'm on the climb back up!

The landings look different,
there's been a lot of redecorating.
My steps are lighter, my eyes clearer.
I carry no bags,
not even finished, fresh laundry—
carrying itself is over.

And I feel my dearth,
the hollow space where once God was.
It was my own doing.

I was going to tear down that old
front bedroom,
completing my extensive renovation,
but I've decided
to leave it just the way it was:
the cedar chest, toy box, 2 single beds,
3 bears, a rabbit, and a monkey—a shrine
to the Lost God.

Epi-self-portait-logue

When we've completed our tour,
I will also need to assure him
that looking at these images
is survivable.
You can get right up close, you can touch them—
you will not disappear, you will not
die, feeling what they meant, knowing
what they mean.
But I'm not saying anyone gets
away unscathed.
No one does.
No one ever does.

Yet, if you perform the right rituals,
occasionally knocking,
occasionally shouting,
Doors *will* open,
And you *will* walk through them.

I am a woman resurrecting—
pushing up wheat
from underground—
learning to be reaper, baker, priest—
healing is holy work.

I am no longer waiting for my parents
to return. I am no longer waiting
for someone-something
beyond myself to rescue me.

I am a woman connecting dots,
testing the air,
melting crayons
into colors I didn't think I could wear.

If you do the right things—
If you do the right things you can learn
to walk with a limp that will barely be noticed.

Then the Exhibit becomes a Retrospective,
        a life's work,
from which the present living of it is liberated.

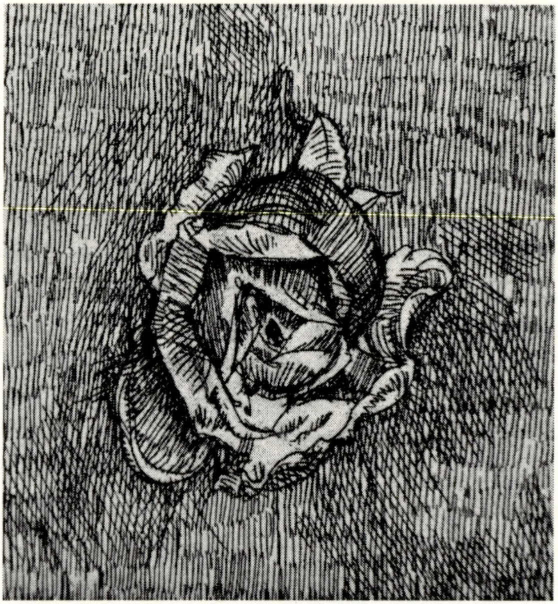

(if you would be) wholly

Cradle your potential.
Ponder the mysteries of your own spirit.
Birth God into the world, again.
Again.

This is required.

Nail your love to the tree of life.
Receive the pain of living deeply.
Do not deny creation your
blood or your laughter.

These also are required.

You are the joy. You are the sacrifice.
This is the law.
(written on your heart, on the stones,
        on the wind)
This is the wholly code.

The Healing

Yes, I am my mother's daughter.
As much I am my grandmother's,
and my great-grandmother's, and my
great-great-grandmother's, on back,
and beyond recollection, beyond where
photographs leave off.
Before there were prints their imprints
were handed down, palm over palm, fist
over fist. I receive my inheritance:
my mother's sorrows which
were her mother's, and
her mother's before her ...

It is for me to uncover the joys—immured
in the depths of blood and being,
swaddled captives, held in trust
for the borning of one generation's
truth-seeker who will
give them back, and pass them on.

an Advent poem

Mother, what was it like
when you waited for me?
When you knew
me only darkly, a
stirring, a quickening
of your body, a nesting—
sometimes a wrenching!
a catch in the breath—
a laden basket you could
not put down ...

Who is it?
did you wonder:
who grows there?
is she like me?
is she *she*?
before I was,
you called me,
and waited with me
and waited for me.

Instruction from the Sea
Or
On the nature of grasping

The Sea speaks to me:
You've got this all wrong. Living
is about giving it up,   letting it go—

Then I rest,
and dream again, and
Hope,
like Prometheus' liver,
grows secretly.

I know about repetition; I know about constancy;
I know about the birth & death and
birth & death of dreams: Today I will
stay upon the shore! Today the Continent
will hold me fast in the union I have so
longed for! Today we will be one,
at last.

[Untitled]

Single pearl

on black velvet

the moon

hovers

spying two

roses

keeping secrets

Beware Aphrodite

Cupid's arrows
are lovers' toys, amusing,
torturously delightful.
No accident though that cupidity
rhymes with—   well.

When Love's Goddess
really wants you,
she comes for you
herself.   No game.
A dark, ecstatic ceremony ...
Your blood, the only oblation.
Your body, the requisite sacrifice.

Stripped—of all you thought you were,
                all you thought love was—
scored,   beaten,   broken,
and raised.
You are food for Heaven.

John O'Groats

The farthest I could get from comfort—
this chilling, blowing outcropped
top of Scotland—I let you
go.

Burial at sea, actually,
on the chopping ferry to Orkney—
the Pentland Firth is known
for tough passage. It was
a small service, clapped
in the chamber of my chest,
as marvelously desolate as
the near-Arctic landscape rising
like tufted backs of whales
on the distance of every side, I
the only attendant, I the presider, I
the advocating spirit: dust to...
gift for a... returned to... etc. etc.
I slid you silently over the side

and you were swallowed immediately
by thoroughly disinterested waves ...

Thousands of miles away you could
only be dimly troubled by a solemnity
you knew tracked my travels—
you will not understand this crossing,
you have no idea where
I have been,
I am not on any map.

Classic

Is it an odd thing to dredge up from memory?
You reading to me in bed... soft, settled,
the hour of love-making domesticated
into the evening by the intervening hours
of dinner & its preparation & its conversation,
clean-up, sorting of tomorrow's clothes
& agendas.   Murder mysteries:
you went through two or three a month,
I would get the isolated chapter
of wherever you were when you stayed
all night.   But I would imagine the rest,
fill in the story, as I probably did with our
lives which came together in more or less
weekly installments—a captivating serial!
Classic plot: one married; brilliant
characterizations; we were hooked.

So here I am, some years beyond the turning
point and Sgt. Havers & Inspector Lynly have
taken form on telly—(American writer posing as
Brit makes lucrative transition from book

to BBC). And when they speak, I hear your
voice low, soft, animated against the tug
of sleep and I feel the side of my face
against your fleshy shoulder, smelling of
powder...   and know that I must grieve
some more my own transition, my own story
of murder & mayhem in which you played
the villain and I the classic unsuspecting
victim that so frustrates the attentive reader
that she shouts aloud, Watch out!
Can't you see what's coming?

I'm usually so good at the game: before anyone
else, I know it's the shy brother-in-law who
stands to inherit after all, or the kindly neighbor
harboring a terrible secret, or when
it really is the butler.
I didn't see the clues; classic.
Perhaps I thought, unconsciously, that if I
refused to figure it out, the story couldn't
END

Crime Scene

"Her fingerprints
are all over your emerging
libidinal architecture—
window sills and door knobs
where she snuck in and just
as deftly slipped out again are covered—
certain cross beams and holding
walls clearly exhibit
prosecutable evidence.
Do you wish to press charges?"

I feel my 12-year-old body
pressed to her tall adult frame
inside the darkness of the equipment
room adjacent to the gym— I always
offer to help, hoping no one else
will— her arms come from
nowhere and I stand within them
unable to move, breathe— I want
to run and I want to turn about to
put my arms around her (a real

embrace! It's what I've dreamed
about for a year— it's the secret
that passes between us when we brush
against each other never really by
accident)— but I do neither.

"Ma'm? Do you wish to press charges?"
Do you think you can find her?
I have been looking all my life—
in all the women I've loved for the wrong
reasons— detecting her in their elusive,
unformed, undisclosed need, in their
remote, unpredictable beauty, in their
sense of self blurred behind several
layers of storm windows.

the view from here

this hole
in me you made
catches the wind
whispering moaning
but my architecture
is unthreatened:
this house stands strong
and still— in fact,
this hole provides
an excellent
window
through which
I see so very
very
clearly

God is a River

God is a river
flowing—flowing—eddying
into inlets I chisel in my old stone coat,
seeping into crevices I chip away at, and
chip away at, swirling into the little bays
I shovel with agony and angst into
the banks of my resistance.

Sometimes
God is a flashflood—
sweeping me from my moorings, shouldering
me atop an unexpected rush—flushed and
altered by the drama and the power
of the erosion of what I thought
was so.

But mostly
God is a river, working
quietly, subtly, steadily
at the granite 'round my soul.

Citizen of the Universe

I am a Citizen of the Universe.

I am a Seeker of the One Force.

I am a Listener for the One Voice.
And I am an echo of it
resounding, rebounding
back toward the Source.

I am a white bird
in a blue sky
catching the currents.

Soaring high and higher
in the blue, and the blue
becomes lighter and lighter,
until the white bird merges
with the white at the top of the sky.

Spiritual Direction

Praise to the East
who daily births the light anew,
sweet-hot and loving labor—

Praise to the South
who sheds and sends her warmth abroad
and carries the Southern Cross—

Praise to the West
who cradles the close of day,
sighing it soft to sleep,
ribboned in gray and vermillion—

Praise to the North
who stirs the whirring globe,
axis-anchored, fixed point
in heaven's perpetual procession.

Summons

It is the most human of acts:
the somber assembling
for death.
The summons in our bones,
carrying the question in our pockets,
we trail in the ancient procession
toward
                    a boundary
                    that suddenly gave way—
                    an unpredictably porous wall.

We catch ourselves in our handkerchiefs,
sidle close to each other like
the insouciant animals we wish we were
and press our eyes to the inscrutable vision—
something
moves
                    at the periphery,
                    disappearing under brush—

A River of Knowing

There is a river
of Knowing.

All are called.
All may drink.

Drawn by some deep
instinct, disclosed or un-

Some take a drop on their lips,
others gulp unutterable draughts,
some wash sleep from their eyes

All are called.
All are welcome.

Some are not thirsty,
others bring no ladle,
some find the taste unpleasing,
some do not trust the well-spring.

O mortal,
take a spoon
and measure the volume
of your soul.

Wilderness

You called me out
of the wilderness of my own aridity.
And you said, be numbered
among those who are mine—
serve my servants,
love my lovers—
Be still; I am indeed.

I went up to your mountains
and glimpsed on each a fainting
ray... a mist ... a shadow ...

So I am haunted now—
glancing out windows,
turning over my shoulder,
watching in my sleep.

Afterword

Several years ago I put a folder I had titled Singing at the Center in my file drawer. Why I titled it that I am not sure. But I thought, at the time, it would be for future poems that would fit that title. Now I think I "knew"—intuited—that someday I would be singing at my center.

I anticipated my psychological healing. I had spent some 20 years in therapy (with some stop outs), with the same therapist who was very good at what she did and fairly unconventional. On the outside I looked fine. My friends and acquaintances perceived me as intelligent, social, artistic, responsible, and good at my teaching job. But inside was a different matter. No one saw this but my therapist. I didn't want to live, and I didn't want to die: the ultimate dilemma. I thought of committing suicide often but never attempted it because I was terrified of death.
I desired an afterlife but didn't believe in one.

I had a provocative relationship with a blue-robed figure; my therapist called these experiences *eidetic visions*. Whatever they were, they occurred mostly 1985–1988. That is what my book *The Debris of the Encounter* is partly about. After that time period, I occasionally had something like them. In these last several years, they have tended to come during meditation.

I have always had an uncomfortable relationship with Christianity. During college, I considered myself an atheist. Several years later after hearing Matthew Fox at La Casa de Maria, a retreat and program center in Santa Barbara, I decided to fight it from within. I have been in the ring with it for many years. Recently, I put my gloves down. There is no fight anymore. I now feel the difference between religion and spirituality; I am a spiritual person. I continue to be a member at St. Michael's Episcopal University Church: it is very small, and one of the aspects I like best is that it reminds me of what the early Jesus-followers were attempting to do, before things became figured out. I go to St. Michael's perhaps three-five times per year, and (so far) I don't get riled up about anything. There is no fight anymore.

I have always been bisexual. Partly, I believe that is because I have spent most of my life trying (psychologically) to get back both my parents. They divorced when I was only six (and my little brother was just two), and we were left with our maternal grandmothers. Our mother visited when she could, and returned for us in about three years. The event of my parents' divorce at my young age is the biggest catastrophe of my life and is what the Divorce Museum, a Child's Perspective, is about. If I hadn't written that, I probably would not be singing at the center now.

My two cats, Isadora (1970-1985) and Cleo (1992-2010) have been very important. I think of them as totemic animals—with all the unconscious spiritual power that implies. The loss of Isadora when I was 33 opened up the chasm—and drove me into therapy. I spent about eight years at it. Having done a lot of work, wanting to be "done"

(one never is, I've learned), desiring to save some money, and feeling okay being in a long-term relationship with a married person (having done work on that, too), I "graduated." Cleo came into my life a few years later.

I had become resigned to many aspects of that married person relationship. I was out of the country for several months (Cleo lived with the neighbors she and her littermates were born to), when all of a sudden the married person cut things off—I could do nothing—I was not able to return to the U.S. for another month. The chasm reopened (in a slightly different way), and a few weeks after my return home, I returned to therapy.

In about the third year, my therapist asked me if I wanted to go deep, with the possibility of "fixing" my life (she didn't use those words but that's what she meant), not just this significant area. It might take years, she cautioned; there will be pain; there are no guarantees; and she did not know what we might find. I thought about this prospect for at least another month or so.

Finally, I said yes.

It was all those things my therapist said it might be.

During that therapy I imagined a fairly stern Medieval guy who lived in my head: he was quiet, read a lot, by candlelight, occasionally looked out his window that was made of leaded glass, and because he lived in my head he lived in a tower-like space, and was in charge; he was my protector. I called him Edgar. (I think this was an outgrowth from the Inner Critic exercise in my book *Writing Your Way to Wholeness*.) Within a year or so, I imagined another figure, a softer, long-bearded, Chinese, robed figure, who had all of my body available but tended to live in my torso; he did a lot of tai ji; his name was Hector.

For a long time they lived separately and never met each other. Last year, when I completed this poetry collection, Edgar came down his ladder, with a younger version of me on his back, and met Hector. They were cordial. They had tea at a table and occasionally Edgar read a newspaper while Hector sipped his tea and looked calmly into the distance. Recently, during meditation imagery, I saw them playing catch with my brain and my heart! I chuckled. If I didn't already believe I had reached my goal, I would have at that point.

I never thought I would experience joy; I thought it was beyond even reaching my goal. But, I did. And I am consistently content. Things changed dramatically inside; things looked pretty much the same on the outside. Only my closest friends and family are aware of the changes. If that catastrophe had not occurred, I might not be the person I am today, whom I like very much.

This year on Good Friday, during my longer than usual meditation, I saw Edgar and Hector and me doing a circle dance, hands clasped; suddenly there was a fourth person in our circle, a very young version of myself. We circle danced, smiled, laughed, and sang at the center.

About the Author

Terre Ouwehand's books include *Writing Your Way to Wholeness: Creative Exercises for Personal Growth* (Resource Publications, 1995); *The Debris of the Encounter: A Recovery of Self* (Resource Publications, 1990); *Voices from the Well: Dramatic Portraits of Extraordinary Women* (MacDonald & Reinecke, 1986).

Her plays include *O'Keeffe*, a one-woman play touring colleges and art museums around the country since 1990 as part of Helena Hale's One-Woman Theater. Ouwehand was a founding member of Actors & Playwrights Theater (APT, 1985-1995) and APT produced her play *Naked Longings* at Santa Barbara's Center Stage Theater (1992). *Are You Still Here?* appeared at Group Repertory Theater in North Hollywood (1991) and as part of Love Songs of the Barbarians (Dramatic Women, 1996); *The Divorce Museum* by DramaDogs at Santa Barbara's Center Stage Theater (2005).

Mass for Our Time is her choral composition with composer John Biggs, premiered by the Ventura Master Chorale (1990), released on CD from Consort Press (2001), performed in New York by The Gregg Smith Singers (1992), in St. Peter, MN by the St. Peter Choral Society & Orchestra (2003), and in Marquette, MI by the Marquette Choral Society (2007).

Terre Ouwehand is an Associate Professor of English at Santa Barbara City College, with an M.A. in Literature & Language Arts from University of California, Santa Barbara, and a B.A. in English from California State University, Fullerton. Terre has designed and continues to teach SBCC's two Sacred Literature courses; she also teaches Creative Writing, Contemporary Dramatic Literature, and Reading & Composition.

She was the Chair of the SBCC English Department, 2002-2008. She has served three times on SBCC's Study Abroad Program in Cambridge, England; she has also served as the Director of the Honors Program. "Living Curriculum" (1988) with her colleague Helena Hale brought her monologues of historical woman into colleges and high schools in Santa Barbara County.

Terre is a frequent workshop leader in the Santa Barbara and Los Angeles areas on topics of sacred texts and creative writing.

Acknowledgements

Trees, Creation IV, Madonna, Citizen of the Universe, God is a River were first published in *The Debris of the Encounter.*

Untitled, Wire & Marble, House on Richardson Rd. were first published in *Writing Your Way to Wholeness.*

The Divorce Museum was first an artists' book; designs by Pamela Zwehl-Burke.
The DramaDogs' theatrical production of the Divorce Museum was in 2005, performed by E. Bonnie Lewis and Ken Gilbert, directed by Erica S. Connell, production & stage management by Michelle Osbourne.

Winter Solstice (the final stanza) appears in the Introduction to *Hymns to the Beloved* by Richard Hooper, Sanctuary Press, 2010.

Vital Signs appears in Solo Café 8&9 (2011), Solo Press.

Printed by Boone Printing and Graphics
Goleta, CA
www.boonegraphics.net